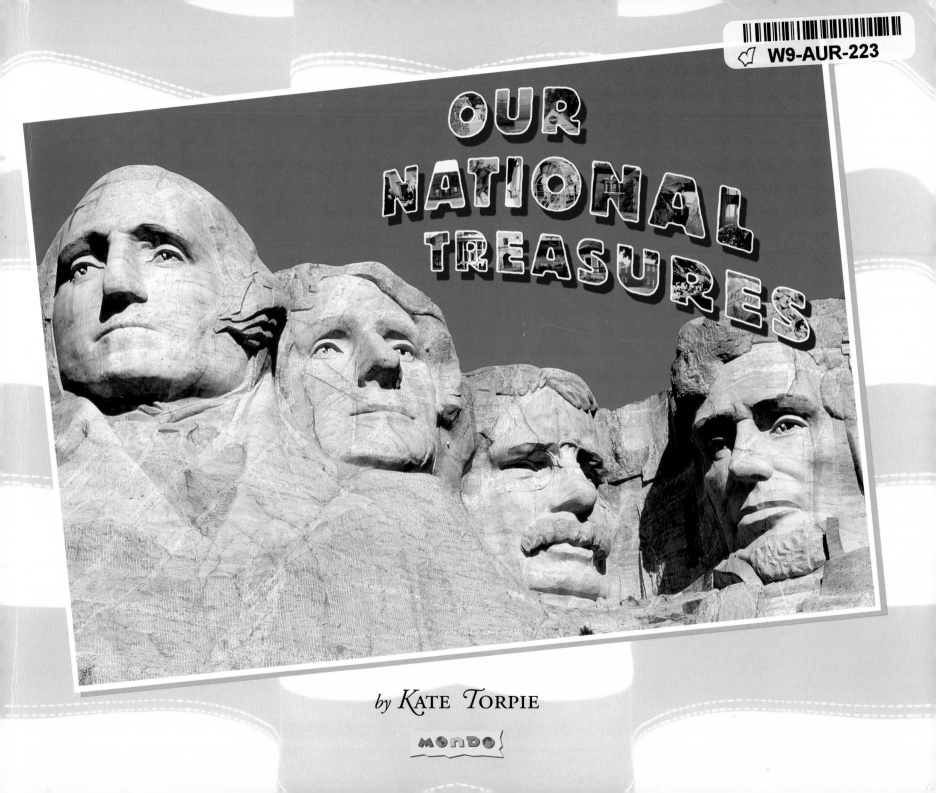

OUR NATIONAL TREASURES

by KATE TORPIE

MONDO

For information contact:
MONDO Publishing
980 Avenue of the Americas
New York, NY 10018

Visit our web site at http://www.mondopub.com

Printed in the United States of America

02 03 04 05 06 07   HC   9 8 7 6 5 4 3 2 1
04 05 06 07   PB   9 8 7 6 5 4 3 2 1

First published in paperback in 2004

Designed by Symon Chow

Library of Congress Cataloging-in-Publication Data

Torpie, Kate, 1974-
    Our national treasures / by Kate Torpie.
        p. cm.
    Contents: Introduction and map -- Independence Hall -- The Statue of Liberty -- The White House -- Plymouth Rock -- The Golden Gate Bridge -- Virginia City -- Mount Rushmore -- The Levi Coffin House -- The Kennedy Space Center -- Poverty Point -- The Alamo -- Cliff Palace -- The Hoover Dam.
    Summary: Text and photographs, both contemporary and historical, provide an introduction to national parks and monuments throughout the nation.
    ISBN 1-59034-191-0 (hc.) -- ISBN 1-59034-042-6 (pbk.)
    1. Historic sites--United States--Juvenile literature. 2. National monuments--United States--History--Juvenile literature. 3. Historic sites--United States--Pictorial works--Juvenile literature. 4. National monuments--United States--Pictorial works--Juvenile literature. 5. United States--Description and travel--Juvenile literature. 6. United States--History, Local--Juvenile literature. 7. United States--Pictorial works--Juvenile literature. [1. Historic sites. 2. National monuments. 3. United States--History, Local.] I. Title.

E159 .T67 2002
973--dc21

2001054438

CONTENTS

INTRODUCTION

Most people have their own treasures—a favorite hat, a best blanket, or maybe a pet. These treasures belong to just one person.

National treasures belong to us all. They are the places or things that tell us something important about our country's past or about our hopes and dreams for the future.

America's national treasures can be found in every part of our country. This map shows where some of them are located. We all share in America's national treasures. Everyone can be proud of them!

America's National Treasures

Alaska

Washington

Oregon

Virginia City
Virginia City

Idaho

Montana

Mount Rushmore
Black Hills
National Forest

North Dakota

Minnesota

South Dakota

Wisconsin

Michigan

Statue
of Liberty
New York Harbor

Plymouth Rock
Plymouth

Vermont

Maine

New Hampshire
Massachusetts

Levi Coffin
House
Fountain City

New York

Rhode Island
Connecticut

Golden
Gate Bridge
San Francisco

Nevada

Utah

Wyoming

Iowa

Nebraska

Colorado

Illinois

Ohio

Indiana

Pennsylvania

New Jersey

Delaware
Maryland

Independence Hall
Philadelphia

California

Kansas

Missouri

Kentucky

West
Virginia

Virginia

White House
Washington, D.C.

Hoover Dam
Black Canyon

Arizona

New Mexico

Oklahoma

Arkansas

Tennessee

North
Carolina

Cliff Palace
Mesa Verde
National Park

Texas

Louisiana

Mississippi

Alabama

Georgia

South
Carolina

Hawaii

Alamo
San Antonio

Poverty Point
Poverty Point

Kennedy
Space Center
Cape Canaveral

Florida

INDEPENDENCE HALL

Philadelphia, Pennsylvania

Independence Hall is a national treasure because important decisions were made there. On July 4, 1776, a group of leaders chosen by the people gathered at Independence Hall. They came to sign the Declaration of Independence. This document told England that America is a free country. The United States of America was born!

Eleven years later, in 1787, a group of lawmakers met at Independence Hall for a special vote. They voted to approve the Constitution. The Constitution gives all Americans fair laws to live by. Today, we follow these same laws.

The Declaration of Independence was signed on July 4, 1776. The Fourth of July is America's birthday.

STATUE OF LIBERTY

New York Harbor

Right in the middle of New York Harbor is the Statue of Liberty. France gave us the statue to celebrate America's centennial, or 100th birthday. The centennial happened in 1876, but the statue was not completed until 1886.

The Statue of Liberty is over 151 feet (46 m) tall. Her mouth is 3 feet (.9 m) across, and her index finger is 8 feet (2.4 m) long. If you climb up 168 steps, you will be inside her crown. You can look out and see New York City and the ships in the harbor.

The Statue of Liberty was the first sight that many immigrants saw in America. For them, and for us today, the torch in her hand stands for freedom.

The statue holds a notebook that reads "July 4, 1776" in Roman numerals.

WHITE HOUSE

Washington, D.C.

The White House is where the President of the United States lives and works. It has rooms for the president's family to live in, offices where people work, and areas for important visitors. The White House also has a bowling alley, a swimming pool, and a movie theater.

Over the years, many presidents have lived at the White House. We honor our presidents by allowing them to live in this national treasure.

This is the president's office. It's called the Oval Office.

rear view of the White House

The White House has 132 rooms—and 32 of them are bathrooms! Its dinner table can seat 140 people.

PLYMOUTH ROCK

Plymouth, Massachusetts

In the year 1620, the Pilgrims left England to find a place where they could be free. They set sail in the ship, the *Mayflower*. Two months later, they came ashore at Plymouth Rock to make their homes in this new land.

Today, Plymouth Rock is smaller than it was 400 years ago. Many visitors have broken off pieces of the rock to keep as their own little treasures. Now, the government protects Plymouth Rock.

The date 1620 is carved into Plymouth Rock.

At Plymouth today, people can see how the town looked in 1620.

The Mayflower *sails to a new land.*

The first Pilgrims land at Plymouth.

Plymouth Rock is protected by this structure.

GOLDEN GATE BRIDGE

**San Francisco,
California**

The Golden Gate Bridge is one of the world's longest suspension bridges. It is almost two miles (3.2 km) long! It took four years to build—between 1933 and 1937.

Because of its name, you might think the bridge is gold or yellow—but it is really orange. The Golden Gate Bridge was named after the waterway it crosses over, the Golden Gate Strait.

The plans for the bridge were drawn by Joseph B. Strauss. He wanted the workers to be safe while they worked on the bridge, so he invented hard hats for them to wear. Mr. Strauss also put a safety net under the bridge. The net saved the lives of 19 workers who fell off the bridge!

The bridge is held up by 80,000 miles (128,748 km) of cable.

The bridge was built between 1933 and 1937.

VIRGINIA CITY

**Virginia City,
Montana**

During the Gold Rush, people hurried westward to find gold. They built new towns wherever they found gold.

In the 1860s, Virginia City, Montana, was home to many gold miners. There were restaurants, food stores, clothing shops, a blacksmith's shop, and a town newspaper.

One day the gold ran out, and everyone left town. Virginia City became a ghost town. Today, the buildings look just as they did in the 1860s. Visitors to Virginia City can see what life was like in the Wild West. People say that if you look under old floorboards, you can still find gold!

Gold miners in Virginia City in the 1860s.

The first school in Montana and the first U.S. Post Office were both in Virginia City.

MOUNT RUSHMORE

**Black Hills National Forest,
South Dakota**

Mount Rushmore is more than just a mountain! It is also a gigantic sculpture of four United States presidents. The four presidents are George Washington, Thomas Jefferson, Theodore Roosevelt, and Abraham Lincoln.

The artist Gutzon Borglum and his workers started carving Mount Rushmore in 1927. They hung from swings almost 6,000 feet (1,828.8 m) above the ground to do their work. At first, they used dynamite and jackhammers to carve away the rock. Then they used tiny hammers. No wonder Mount Rushmore took 14 years to complete!

President Lincoln's mouth is 18 feet (5.5 m) wide.

Each president's face is 60 feet (18.3 m) tall and 20 feet (6.1 m) wide.

LEVI COFFIN HOUSE

**Fountain City,
Indiana**

Slavery is a part of America's history. Many brave people tried to escape it by going to states where slavery was not allowed. Some free people helped runaway slaves escape by hiding them in secret places. Then they led the runaway slaves on secret paths to the next person who wanted to help. This was called the Underground Railroad. The helpers were called railroad conductors.

Levi Coffin and his wife, Catherine, were railroad conductors. They hid runaways in a small room in their attic. They closed its tiny door and pushed a bed in front of the door. No one knew the room was there. If people had found out, the Coffins and the runaway slaves would have been punished.

Today, the Levi Coffin House looks just as it did in 1839. It reminds us of the heroes who stood up for freedom!

Today, visitors can go into the secret room in the Coffins' attic.

The Coffins helped over 2,000 people reach freedom.

KENNEDY SPACE CENTER

Cape Canaveral, Florida

The Kennedy Space Center is home to the United States space program known as NASA. Since 1950, 3,000 spacecraft have been launched from there. In 1969, Apollo 11 blasted off from the Kennedy Space Center and went all the way to the moon. Today, the space shuttles launch and land at the center.

The Kennedy Space Center has a museum where visitors can see historic rockets and space suits. They can peek in at launch control or touch a moon rock. Visitors can watch spacecraft blast off from two giant launchpads.

Visitors can also watch as NASA builds the International Space Station, where astronauts live in outer space.

The new International Space Station will be so large that you won't need a telescope to see it in space!

POVERTY POINT

Poverty Point, Louisiana

This prehistoric landmark is where Native Americans built a village almost 4,000 years ago. Once, as many as 600 Native Americans may have lived at what we call Poverty Point. Today, all that is left of the village are mounds of dirt in a giant half circle. The half circle is almost 4,000 feet (1,219.2 m) across. The largest mound is in the shape of a bird. It is 70 feet tall (21.3 m), 710 feet long (216.4 m), and 640 feet (195 m) wide.

Artifacts found at Poverty Point include beads shaped like birds, arrowheads, tools, and jewelry made with stones that come from far away. These artifacts show that the Poverty Point villagers probably liked birds and traded with people from other parts of what would become America.

Poverty Point today

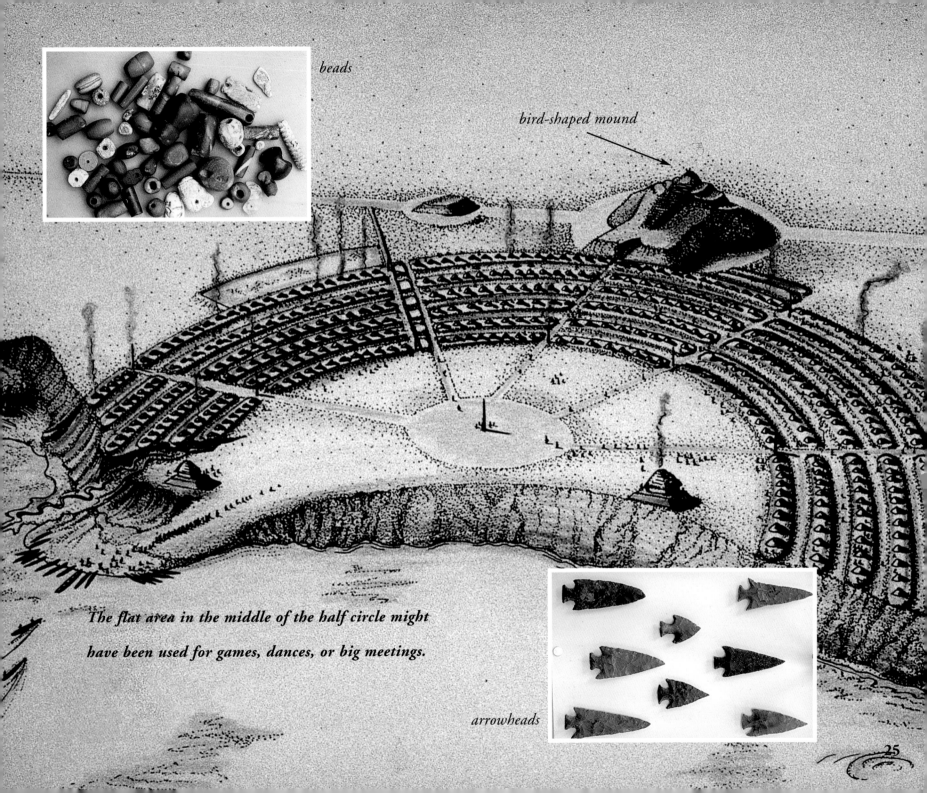

beads

bird-shaped mound

The flat area in the middle of the half circle might have been used for games, dances, or big meetings.

arrowheads

25

ALAMO

San Antonio, Texas

The state of Texas was once a part of Mexico. In the 1800s, the people who lived in Texas wanted to be free from Mexico. In 1836, they fought a terrible battle at a mission called the Alamo. Only 189 Texans were inside the Alamo fighting thousands of soldiers from Mexico. The Texans fought hard, but they lost the Battle of the Alamo.

Losing the Battle of the Alamo made people in Texas want their freedom from Mexico even more. "Remember the Alamo!" they would yell to encourage one another. The army from Texas fought and fought, and at last they won!

Today, the Alamo reminds people of the importance of freedom.

Davy Crockett, an American legend, was one of the soldiers who fought for freedom at the Alamo.

CLIFF PALACE

Mesa Verde National Park,
Colorado

Cliff Palace was the home of the prehistoric Native Americans called the Anasazi. The Anasazi built their homes in large caves high up in the sides of stone cliffs. Cliff Palace is the largest of these homes. It was probably more like an apartment building than a palace.

At some time between the years 1200 and 1300, the Anasazi suddenly left Cliff Palace. It is not known why they left. The Anasazi did not write down their history, but they did leave behind pottery, baskets, blankets made of turkey feathers, and jewelry made of silver and turquoise. That makes Cliff Palace a treasure of information about America's past!

Cliff Palace has 217 rooms.
It was probably home to 250 people.

Anasazi pottery

HOOVER DAM

**Black Canyon,
Nevada**

The Colorado River used to flood every few years. Every time it flooded, it ruined crops for miles around—but then the Hoover Dam was built! The dam was named after President Herbert Hoover, and it is one of the largest dams in the world. It holds back the waters of the Colorado River.

The Hoover Dam is made of giant blocks of concrete. The dam stands 726 feet (221.3 m) high and contains 840 miles (1351.9 km) of pipes. When the dam was finished in 1935, the water it blocked formed a lake. That lake is now called Lake Mead. It is over 100 miles (161 km) long.

The Hoover Dam took less than five years to build and used enough concrete to make a sidewalk around the Earth!

GLOSSARY

Anasazi   the Navaho name for the prehistoric people who are believed to be the ancestors of many Southwestern Native American tribes

artifact   an object from the past

dam   a wall that blocks the flow of water in a river or stream

ghost town   a town that no longer has anyone living in it

immigrant   a person who is moving or has recently moved to a new country

liberty   freedom

mission   a kind of church

prehistoric   from a time before people wrote information about themselves

ruin   what is left of a place that has been left alone for a very long time

sculpture   a work of art that has been carved or built

suspension bridge   a roadway that hangs from cables and towers to allow people or things to cross over something

Underground Railroad   a secret system of people and places that helped slaves in America travel from the states where slavery was legal to the free states